08082

GH00888855

EDDA COMMUNITY LIBRARY
Monday - Friday 10.00am - 4.00pm
Saturday 10.00am - 1.00pm
Tel: 01704 578003 · Email: eddaarts@btconnect.com
Part of the Bridge Inn Community Farm Ltd.

Into Hiding

—————————— ○ ——————————

Brian Wake

HEADLAND

First published 1993 by
Headland Publications
38 York Avenue, West Kirby,
Wirral, Merseyside. L48 3JF

A CIP record for this book is available from the British Library.
ISBN
0   903074   81   8

Acknowledgements are due to the publications and programmes in
which some of these poems first appeared:

Ambit, Ideas In English (Mary Glasgow Publications), BBC TV
"Closedown", *Smoke,* BBC Radio Merseyside, BBC Radio 4, *Sol
Magazine, Tears In The Fence, Brando's Hat, Envoi, Die Horen*
(Germany) *New Poetry 3* (Arts Council).

*Headland gratefully acknowledges
financial assistance fom North West Arts Board.*

Printed by Nichols Print, Heswall, Merseyside.

CONTENTS

for Janet
(after so long)

INTO HIDING

Hiding from me at bedtime, my daughter
sneezes and giggles from inside the wardrobe.
I wonder where she is, I act. Pretending
not to see her four small fingers
clutching the door.
But, fearing the dark far more
than she does me, she surrenders.
I gasp in mock surprise.
Soon she will be sleeping.

In Germany once
whole families hid in cupboards
while friends pretended not to see.
But forty years on, most would say
forget, forgive, let ancient horrors be.

Me? I am reminded tonight
of the mother who, on hearing footsteps
on the stairs, hurried her children
into hiding; four hearts thumping
in a wardrobe.

Like mine, perhaps her daughter
would have giggled had she sneezed.
Sneezed and giggled, giggled and sneezed,
sneezed away four lives.

I smothered her, says a broken woman,
so the others might survive.
It was Thursday, the ninth,
in nineteen thirty nine,
November, I remember, she says,
thinking even then
how all her little movements
were as earthquakes when
matched against the stillnesses
to come.

AUNT

Fifteen years ago she was taken,
smelling of cheap wine, her fingers
brown with Woodbines, away.

Fifteen years ago, taxied off -
wireless, handbag, a hat thrown on
(hoop-la'd onto a sad head).

A sight to set the curtains trembling,
to let the whole street talk for months.

Off our hands, she marched the corridors
of her new home, throwing space
behind her with her one good arm
- the bad, a lance to poke at all
of which she disapproved.

And always (during visits),
through the clumsy shapes of smoke
escaping past her port-pink lips,
"I'm coming home," she'd splutter,
"home," she'd say, "and tell your mother that."

The sort that lives forever.
And now in a cold room
my mother and I stand; me -
fixed upon the bloodless look,
the fingers Woodbine brown;
she - wanting just to tuck her in,
to straighten the dead sister out.

SNAPSHOT

Correctly centered, well boxed in,
we stand, my brother and I, in a garden.
He, upright, braving the hard light,
his hair watered neat. Me,
my hand saluting for shade,
one sock down - a sight!

And of what are we dreaming
as we stand just a summer or two
past the shudders of war?
He, perhaps, about the games
to play inside broken homes,
the gunner-gouged streets,
the disorder of debris. Me,
the little tag-along, of simply
picking up the fun he never had.

Parts of us both have faded
into a landscape long since altered.
The grey of us into the grey
of grass and stone.
And out of this soiled snapshot
we have grown, my brother and I,

from brothers into men.

ADRIFT

My father talks of being twenty
days in an open boat. Adrift.
My father and others.

Wartime and the ocean
was a blood-slick
clinging to continents.

They had been hit
and only the dead escaped
the long days
measured by the turning
of the boat beneath
a cruel sun. Each day
a million years
of cracked tongues
along the chalk of teeth.

He remembers giving up,
that his final thoughts
were of crookedly beautiful
backyard walls and thin
but glorious lines of smoke
from little chimneys.
In winter, rivers of gusting snow
down white and moaning lanes.
In summer, flowers and things
they wished they had done or said.

He recalls them believing
themselves to be dead
yet each alive to mourn
his own death.

My father talks of the years
having flown, of being
twenty days adrift.
His garden is a blizzard
of white roses.

HORIZONS

Home from sea and this time
home for good, paid off and spent,
        my father
walks around and looks for things
to do; for wood to stain,
for clocks to wind and cups
to swill the tea leaves from.

For much of the time
he is sleeping. Dark eyes
locked away but quick
to catch the sudden silver
of a turning fish or, after weeks
of oceans, moisten at the bomb smashed
Mersey skyline, see again
his city smouldering,
its streets and houses gone.

Seventy four and moored
for good in the calm of home,
        my father
plants his sea-time clues
in bits of conversation. Teasing
us with nights in New Orleans.
Of shipwrecks in the Gulf
that fizzle out mid-tale.

Around the quiet house,
he looks for little things to do;
for doors to bolt
or potted plants to trim,
a wall to paint horizons on.

GOING DOWN

Horses drum across the TV screen,
dicing the damp turf, foaming with sweat.
The one my father's done is racing now.
Jumping like a stag, he says, and moving well.

Over his specs, his 'fancy' - fixed within
a win-you-bastard stare - skips on
but then mistimes a fence and crouches to a fall.

In Montreal one time, my father says,
as if to climb back into brighter thoughts
than a pension picked away by bets gone down,
the skipper, second mate (old Charlie what's
his name) and me were in a bar....
And once in New Orleans another time....
And once in Cuba....

Bought your mother jewellery, I think.
And you boys shirts, those sleeveless ones
and records, Lena Horne....

The winning jockey doffs his cap
and yanks the saddle from his steaming horse.
Behind the words, my father strains
against his loss and folds his paper
into small and smaller squares.

SHORTCUTS

Living, as we did, a little
out of town, my mother always knew
the quick ways back from what had been
her home; her mother's place,
to where with us she had removed.

Knew all the shortest ways,
the lanes that dipped and rose,
the cinder path that bumped us
out of dreams and into starlight.
Wheeled us home, she did,
and through the darkness faintly singing.

From her house now,
I push my way to mine.
And on the lanes and newly levelled paths,
meander like a drunk but purposely.
Not to delay arrival
but to take again what were
my mothers quick ways home
and sing .

BURIED TREASURE

Died at sea, he did. Something to do
with ulcers. Buried at Capetown.
The snapshots show a quiet grave,
some company reps and wreaths,
some shipmates, stewards, sparks,
but no 'old man'.

And no old man himself, yet dead
and buried miles away from home.

As kids, in 1955, we hardly felt
the space my sea-going grandfather's
death had made. But rather fancied
how they'd taken him ashore,
how chevroned, heaving oars
had pushed the sea behind,
and a long boat's keel had gashed
and scarred the saltwhite sands of Africa,
and how our mother's father's corpse
was buried treasure
miles and miles away.

HIGH WINDOWS

No mines but always coal;
the smell of coal
and the smack in the mouth
of gas across black hills.
And, further on, squat dockside
cranes, their lines spun out
into the grey Mersey.

Bootle this,
backstreet upon backstreet
upon backstreet and gaps
like missing teeth.
A hard-case place, proud
of its bomb scars,
of its fires in blitztime.

And here, from the highest
windows, above the sudden squares of grass,
the speckle of fog-lights poking
through the shapes of streets, I am
drawn to absences,
to spaces in the air
where buildings pressed and steam
blew from slithering trains once,
where songs from pubs and parlours
rose and burst, and slow men
tugged horses, ringing hooves,
over grinding lanes.

LODGER

From who knows where
my grandmother's lodger came;
a sunset-ginger perm,
rich-voiced and warm as August nights.

From who knows where, and yet
her being there was holiday for us;
all hell let loose and toast in bed
and torchbeams on the bedroom walls.

Her stories, from downstairs,
would light our rooms (imaginations
spun in harmony with hers).
And we, against a creaking banister,
would hush to hear her travelogue,
and crouching closer, half-asleep,
would misconstrue the scraps of facts
picked up along her way;
her worldliness, her haughty air,
and all so thinly stretched like string
that bound her little bits of life.

Her leaving was my first real Autumn.
Kicking space into deep, dead leaves,
I followed the vaguest sound
of what might have been her voice.
Above all, stretching tallest
over shopping crowds and bus queues,
anywhere and everywhere to see, perhaps,
the sunset-ginger perm slip down
behind anonymous facescapes.

KEPT SIMPLE

Eighty seven, she was, or eight,
quite deaf and yet we'd bawl
our names to her as if to rouse
some sleeping thing,
identify our kids and muddle
all her sense of time.

Like curling snapshots kept
to weave the thread of generations,
we kept her. We, my family;
she, a simple woman - mind jammed
in between the turn of centuries.

As kids ourselves, we'd heard
how she was pulled
from bomb-swept streets and through
the heart-storm of her mother's death .

At forty five an orphan,
taken in and kept until today
when, cutting threads at eighty odd,
she prised the centuries apart.

SMALL SQUARE

And here, he said, right here,
standing in a small square
against a new brick wall,
his hands reshaping rooms.

Here, he said, his eyes rising
step by slow step, head tilted
at invisible stairs.
This, he said, is where they lay,
caught in the downpour of iron
and stones but calm beneath
a glowing sky and the hum of aircraft.
And here, he said, right here,
his fingers following brickshapes.

From the imagined edges
of his special space, we watch
my cousin pushing back through
more than forty years
to rouse the sleepers there.

As casually as home for tea,
my cousin's heart rebuilds
his mother's home
and moving through the night
he goes to her
and here and there
from room to room to room.

OPEN FIRE

I wonder did one finger pick at dust
or a bruised eye open on to rough stone
whether any flickering thoughts
quickened towards conclusions.

I just couldn't bring her round,
my grandmother had said,
slapping her own knuckles as she dug
back into blitztime.

And there we were, three kids hearing this
before an open fire, gases hissing
from the hot coal and each of us
seeing dockyards burning in the grate,
our evening playstreets pricked with sparks.

I wonder did one finger pick at dust,
I thought, a closing eye see light
beneath the door.

SMALL OPENINGS

As able as anyone to unpuzzle
the maze of streets,
find shops, say this please,
that please, thank you, I am
and maybe more so.

And yet the corridors stretch endlessly
and blocks of light, stacked
against windows, bar my way.
Outside, the tramcar sparks along
grey lanes, slicing the mist.
I see this through small openings.

Each morning a woman enters my room
to hold my wrist gently, tempting me
with food and drink.
But for the dry ache that groans
inside my belly, I would resist;
because of it, I eat.

At night I crouch, dark against dark
walls, darker still than blindness.
Again she comes.
Outside in the dark room,
she looks for me.
She forgets my name and is angry.
Cowering, I see all this
through the very smallest of openings.

FORTY WINTERS

After the snow,
after long quiet days of snow
and the shock of cold glass
uncurtained on to silent swirling
and altogether softer streets.

After all this,
the yellow grass
and the last rooftop-sliding-snowpile
thudding on to green-again lawns,
and cars again sluicing the grooves,
dark snowdregs spraying the pavements,
footprints spreading into dark pools.

This is my fortieth snowtime,
forty winters of storms and stillnesses,
and the times (between the falling
and the thaw) growing briefer,
and snowspots left unspoilt
- more difficult to find.

SUMMER (IN ME)

Summer (in me), the ice softens
and the heart hurts less.
Such a curious Spring has passed,
so little grew, so few lives stirred.

Winter too was strange,
the sudden change from green to grey,
the sudden switch from fire to ash,
from hurrying streams to ice.

I move very little these days
(and cautiously), sit a good deal
unravelling the years
that have begun to twist around me.
I miss much, mourn so many moments
that have gone - the green today,
tomorrow the grey.

Passing through the seasons in between,
I wait for Summer
and the Summer (in me) waits to interest me
by passing.

WHAT AWAITS

Go on ahead, you said, and I
shall follow. Take the surest path.
Move quickly now, careful
on stream stones, steady
at the river's edge. For what awaits
is worth a hundred journeys such as this.

Go on ahead.
And this now more than half my life ago.
So how can I not doubt
that you are just a little way
behind me yet.

TAKING STEPS

Next Summer we shall sit, eating bread
and cheese from a bag, on the warm steps
around the Piazza della Signoria.

Recalling today and this brown garden
knotted inside a year of tangled grass,
and threaded into a dead stillness
by the webs that spun each dark corner.

Recalling too the directions we planned.
Like Generals, with canes, scratching strategies
into the desert sand, we shall remember
sketching, from the steps in Florence,
dreams on the hard soil in this dead garden here.

Our eating done, we shall take whatever steps
will lead us to the highest places above the city.
Seeing, as we climb, a tapestry of tended gardens
behind us - gardenias high as houses
and grass brushed smooth by steady winds.

No tangled webs shall weave around us then,
but only the very brightest lights
shall spread their gold
into the underneath of things.

COMING THROUGH

After the storm here,
it has been quite impossible
to move without falling against debris,
without the fear of being
impaled on the (white as shark's teeth) spikes
of what, just yesterday, were simply branches
bent beneath the tons of buds. Poised
close to the yellow/green of spring.

After this, where to be
that is familiar, to tread
that will not open like a wound.

Today I dreamed spaces where you had been,
absences, dark shapes in the sunlit places.
After the storm, no sounds,
mountains upturned, rivers gone....

But, oh my beautiful you, not us,
and I am kissing light back into your eyes.
I am holding your hand now!

IN BETWEEN LIVES

In and out of the cold rain,
and out there, car sounds
like the flight of arrows,
like the movement of those herds
of muscle that heave against
the rapid-flowing miles of African rivers,
splash upstream to new and hitherto
untrodden hunting places....
I am almost at home
amongst the bits and pieces, the odds
and ends of suitcase-able things.

And thinking of you there.
In, perhaps, out of rain yourself.
And alone too, with your own
arrow-swishing dramas, your own
particular throng of beasts
battering the river bed.

Alone, and only thoughts between us
that we might be together in the end.

ACCESS

Watching at the door
for the first fall of snow,
my children stand aside as I visit.

In Bristol, they tell me,
the drifts are doorstep high,
and not one single engine driver
has the balls to set his train
spellbindingly against
the windscreen-rattling storm.
And then again, in Cuckoo
Land the sun is shining still.

My time with the kids these days
is mostly spent on planning out
what next to do, what days are best
and where we all might go.
Outside, the sky swells mauve and grey
with snow that will not fall.

Still they watch and I watch them,
and home is not at all
where-ever you hang your hat.

WONDERFUL PAIN

And when it is over,
what will they make of this,
the children.
Saying, perhaps, how they missed
the years in between,
the days of dancing.

And how he danced and danced
and danced away,
and paused to see us
standing there, they'll say,
then danced and danced
and danced again,
lightly on a patch of love,
that wonderful pain.

SOMEONE LIKE ME

Someone not unlike me, someone
very like me is at a kitchen window.
Someone with eyes like mine looks out.

The first birds have gone
and only the late ones bounce
from stone to stone, peck morsels.

Behind a frosted bathroom glass
a pink shape moves, and someone
much like me is watching.

From his window, on the backyard
wall, reflections prowl.
From his opening kitchen door,
a sudden dawn of houselight.

Someone just like me has moved
outside, has caused the birds to go,
is shaking the dew from what flowers there are.

Like me, he is at home among the bricks,
the chimneys and the whiff of breakfasts
over back-entry walls.

Someone not unlike me, someone
very like me is resting at a window sill.
Our eyes meet and one of us is weeping.

COUNTRY DANCING (AS THERAPY)

There is nothing to be frightened of, she said,
but come along and lie down on the bed.
We spoke of country dancing and of how
so very sad it was to have to dance alone,
to move in time with no-one's steps and music but your own.

But there is nothing to be frightened of, she said,
and come, my dear, and lie down on the bed.

And country dancing was the only time I ever moved.
A solitary shuffler, shadow-partnered, I improved,
danced the days away from wall to wall
and although I often stumbled they had taught me how to fall.

But when the dancing ended I could always hear
the voice that told me there was nothing there at all to fear.

There is absolutely nothing to be frightened of my dear.

DON'T LOOK, JUMP

Long before
I knew about the sea
or of those creatures
darting in its heart,
I would wade or swim
far out, crashing like a wave
myself through waves,
would circle the dancing bouys
and return, glistening,
to the shore....

Now,
having learned just a little more
about tides and all
the hidden depths,
the vicious ways of fish,
I stand shivering and safe
where the sea is weakest -
one foot scouting for dangers.

YOUR LAST SPRING

Awkwardly down on the lawn,
you ruffled the soil to poke the limp shoots in
and set them off.

I watched.
Your wife brought drinks outside. We drank,
 and tea-steam puffed along with what you had to say.

The sun stayed late that day. Held on
as though to give you extra time and light
to get things done.

That summer your garden failed.
A doomgrey stain along the chain of luscious lawns.
Nothing you had tended grew,
while surgeons fought to scrape the fateful tumours
from your spine.

TALKING OF BATTLES

Sooner or later the cup-clink
is the tick-tick-tick of faraway guns.
I crunch my biscuit and think
of boots marching into gravelly towns;

think not of Ceasars, Bonaparte,
but of the (yes sir) boys who ached for home;
marched not on stomachs but on their hearts;
were cattled in thousands yet each alone.

In times of hardship, war, men share
what little bits they have, you tell me.
Smoke? A cigarette? Here
catch. Air seemed green with gas
the sky was dull with clouds of poison smoke.
I lay in ditches, lay in hell.

We placed out trust in greater men
than we were. Woodbines, they were all we had.
The landscape sort of twitched and every now and then
a tree, or flower, bird or man - fell dead.

The next one won't be fought that way,
you tell me, somehow, sadly. No, a quick
decision; rush of burning air and blinding
flash and that'll do the trick.

STONES

Stones are surfaces, nothing else.
They cannot break
except into a thousand stones. Smooth
as the air that oozes
from the space we take, sharp
as splintered bone,
or the crooked flicker of lightning.
Our touch is their structure.
They exist only on the tips of fingers,
the tips of tongues.

Stones are the shape of water.

As warm as ripe sun distorted
on the mirror of seas, or cold
as moon-steel speckled
against the dark falling snow.
Colder than indifferent eyes.

Stones are the decisions the eye makes.

Their taste is of salt wind on burst lips,
the flavour of hard earth.
Their sudden dryness
is a mouthful of cloth. Stones
are fog-tone. They have it's silence.
The invisibility fog creates
is that of stones.
And to look is to discover
stones are everywhere.   Knowing.   Sensing.

Touch them and they move.   They survive
by being less than living things.

KILLING TIME

In from the rain, a sudden rush
of flower bending drops, they come
dripping exclamation marks
from room to room.

At windows hoot like hell
through towels, these men,
to see their storm caught mates
come thundering down the rapid
pathways, past rockery and bowling-green
- a river now, its breakers beating
on abandoned woods.

In from blistering flower-beds left unmade,
the bulging hedgerows heaving to be cut,
the litter of leaves, the half-mown turf,
the sweat. They sit, thanking Christ
for the rain, in steaming coats,
hot tea and fingers stiff with cigarettes.

Killing time, they chisel boots
from blocks of soil, these men, each one
scraping the surface of the next
and nodding with the urgent rain.

WAITING FOR MUSIC

At the table with paper, I moved
a line or two around the shape of you,
played outlines against planes
to raise you from the white.

Behind your head a window was to frame
the hills of Malvern sharpened into houses,
streetstones were to echo sky light
and the lines of smoke and rooftops
were to be so very softly toned
with lampglow, silvered by this cold
November.

Instead
I am waiting for music and the view
from where I sit is of a window
in a window across a narrow road in Bootle,
a corridor of forms half hidden
by the angles of the light.
Receding images reflected and reflected,
each casting back the smaller image
of itself and, inside that, myself
at my table with paper
thinking of you at yours - more than 40 now and still
quite well and waiting also for the same
music.

FINE

Driving from Bootle to Kidderminster,
counting not so much the miles
as the years that have passed
since we last met.

And thirteen later, there you are
with one tooth gone, less hair
and a once familiar voice less clear.

Why here, I ask, and are you here for good.
Why not, you croak, your worn hands dark
against that half forgotten face.

The house looks nicely out onto
a green space. I have a fine wife,
fine kids and a fine friend indeed,

and the local general shop,
a stone's throw off, stocks everything
I need

GRASS

Not to be outdone by the man
who held that in another life
he had been nothing more
than foot-tracks after snow,
I too know the acres of a pinhead.

For I have been a single spine of grass.
Not shoots defying feet or hooves,
or needles pricking jealously a lovers,
but only grass - and one who learned
to weave around the wind.

I made no play for prominence,
nor contemplated grassness,
checked my head was always level
with the rest, and had no name but grass.

Though, sometimes, storms
have forced me down to earth,
I have spread myself onto the soil,
have waited, ground down, harmed
but never broken.

MURDER

From among the quiet ruins
of Summer, the plaited whips
of leafless vine,
the corpse of a spider
spinning from the gallows
of it's web, the hush of leaves
shifting crisply;
a sudden cat
has roared onto a thrush.

In a scuffle of screaming
brown and black and blood,
its dozen rapiers slice
and plunge. The bird's wild eyes
meet only teeth, wings are spread
on claws.

Its murder done,
the cat comes home for food.
Beneath the warm dead thrush
the worms are turning.

GONE FISHING

Dragging the local pond
for whatever moved beneath
it's cross-hatched reeds,
or skimmed its surface
to the safer banks;
nine years old and there
she blows, we'd howl, we hunters,
our laundry basket catch-all
hurled to the deep
and hauled by the ropes back in again.

Pearl Harbours and Hiroshimas
were these to those beneath.
Our basket blasting tidal waves
that would pitch burst creatures
here and there;
frogs into trees
and fishes in the air.

But mostly mud we dredged
and hurrying things
that did as well on land.

Yet always there, among the oozing
pond bed. silver flickerings
would light our eyes,
and jars with strings around their necks
would hold our prisoners, our prize.

BROKEN THINGS

Doing out the house,
reshaping a room,
there are many things to go:

a record sleeve
without a record in,
a can of white gloss paint
now yolk-shade bound in skin,
foresaken toys, rusted knives,
a clock that stopped in 1965,
the Queen's cracked face
distorted on a plate,
a chest of drawers
the shelves of which are lined
with Churchill-bulldog shapes
and news of victory, an end
to wars, a kind of peace at last.

From out of all the spaces
I am making in this room,
dust puffs and pauses
into cloud and like dark snow
falls softly onto broken things.

AT THAT AGE

At that age, we are,
when falling means long moments
on the ground, crawling for help
or slowly straightening into pain.

In spite of this, our Malvern snow-walks
were risks we had to take
to get to all the highest places
on the hills.

Surprising most of all
was how unsteady you had grown,
and how that son of yours
could scale the perilous crags
and skate from height to height.

Back home, we dwelt on it for hours,
talking proudly of our bruises
and about the pain, of falling.
A price, we agreed, well paid
for a white unusual day;
for the sight of Brueghel-patchwork towns
from high up on the slippery hills.

Well and warm into the rest
of the day, we talked and talked -
our damp old boots hardening
before the open fire.

JUST ANYTHING

You'd have liked this one, old man.
Either nodding in and out of sleep
behind your Daily Mail,
or later from the artery bursting
agonies of your last weeks;
have enjoyed this piece, old man
now two years dead.

'O Mio Babbino Caro,' someone sings.
Puccini. And I imagine you'd have said
just anything to speak the catch
out of your throat, or avert your head
to hide from us those tell tale tears.

DARK REFLECTIONS

Nothing to come down for,
said the man on the high ledge,
nor reason to live.   Transfixed,
we watched as he leaned towards the edge.

Behind his head a window swelled
with clouds - distorted dark reflections.
And, suddenly, "Jump," yelled
one of us in the crowd .

Again, again and again, he did.

FOUR DOGS

Four days,
they said, a dead man
- frozen where he died -
staring into the eyes
of those he had forgotten.

Four days dead
and yet had seemed alright
last night moving about
his room, they said,
his head held downward
as if in searching...

For days
his dogs had watched with him.
No food but dust
and a jagged fist clenched
inside their bellies.

At last they smelt
their master's bones,
at last began devouring him.
One a limb, another
growled on veins, another
poked away the eyes
and snorted as it fed,
while the fourth
(his special one) they said,
tore apart the heart.

GARDENER

Winter was the time for taking stock.
Cursing the ice for its cruelties,
he would spend his shortened days
slicing ways through the snow.

Evenings, a silent man brushing specks
from pages with the back of his hand,
sparing the beetle in its search for heat,
noting the tap of twigs on glass,
wind sounds and the rush of gas
from scorching coals.

Though mostly still, he would soar.
Though silent, orchestras boomed.

In the cold moments of light,
he would trundle the park paths.
A summer man crouched against a hostile season.

Without flowers to tend,
he would fill cracked flags with cement
and his time brushing up the fragments
of autumn poems.

FLOWERS IN THE PARK

Something quite erotic about raw shoots
piercing the soil   -   tricked
by a frostless month, a mild November,
Something tender but rude
about the rigid, quivering buds.

And through the last crisp sheets of leaves,
the thin, pink twigs are poking,
each tip a tense projection
twitching to touch its inch of light.

Something quite outrageous
about damp earth swelling,
trees too, and the thrust and pink
of petals unwinding, opening
slowly into deep and gorgeous flowers
in the park.

DOING NOTHING

That you can sit
all day, you say,
amazes; doing little
but watching
the cat, the sunlight
spread across the floor,
flowers in a vase.

And surely there
are times
when you would rather
take to the hills,
be dazzled
by quick birds
in flight, see woodlands
where the green is thick
with living things,
and the breezes,
softly moving on the waters,
are a kind of song.

It is, you say,
so strange how you can seem
content to sit so long.
The cat's tail
drums the beat of a bad dream.
She turns. Sunlight sprawls
against the wall.
The flowers in the vase
do nothing.

BIOGRAPHICAL NOTE

BRIAN WAKE *has been involved with poetry for more than twenty-five years. During that time his work has been published and broadcast both here and abroad. In the 1960s and 1970s he set up a series of small presses and was responsible for publishing the poetry magazines,* Matrix, Asylum *and* Driftwood Quarterly. *He later went on to launch the* Driftwood Poets Series - *limited editions of poetry booklets by new unpublished poets.*

Into Hiding *is Brian Wake's first book of poems since 1980. Previous publications include:* Ghosts of Myselves *(Second Aeon, 1969),* Stars *(Driftwood, 1972) and* Doing Nothing *(Windows, 1980).*